# The Sky Goes on Forever

## Dr. Diana Prince

AuthorHouse™
1663 Liberty Drive
Bloomington, IN 47403
www.authorhouse.com
Phone: 1 (800) 839-8640

The cover photo and all interior photos are used with permission of Getty Images.

This book is printed on acid-free paper.

ISBN: 978-1-7283-2062-5 (sc)
ISBN: 978-1-7283-2063-2 (hc)
ISBN: 978-1-7283-2061-8 (e)

Library of Congress Control Number: 2019910352

Print information available on the last page.

Published by AuthorHouse 07/23/2019

authorHOUSE®

# Table of Contents

# WAKING UP

The sunlight falls across the spread,
in sunny patches on my bed.

A bird flies by the window glass.
Outside my Dad is mowing grass,

And everyone's awake, I see,
in all the world, except for me.

How warm and cozy it all seems—
I close my eyes for one more dream.

# FLIGHT OF THE BALLOONS

Into the sky
I send my favorite balloons
in pink and blue and white—

I send them on their way
To dazzle in the light.

And higher than the day,
Like stars, they lift up
Out of sight.

Over the rooftops they drift on
And brighter than the day,
They cross the oceans
to the world where other children play.

I send these balloons
to say we all are loved—
Each child, every one.

On this bright day,
I send my balloons
like wishes to the sun.

# TAKING MY DOG FOR A WALK

I take my dog out for a walk;
He never listens when I talk.

He likes to pull this way or that,
Or chase the neighbor's yellow cat,

And if some children pass our way,
He always wants to stop and play.

If we go on the river path,
He wants to stop and take a bath,

And if the postman pats his head,
He might go home with him instead.

And when the walk is almost through,
He wants to chase a squirrel or two.

At home he jumps up in my lap.
By then, I'm ready for a nap.

# MY BRIGHT YELLOW BOOTS

I got new yellow boots today,
the color of the sun,
Bright yellow, slick and bright—
Ready to jump and run.

They look like little yellow ducks,
And every time we race,
My friend says that he thinks
"They can be seen from outer space."

## BUTTERFLY

What are you,
little flying thing—

In brilliant colors
like a king?

Through bluest skies and hills of green,
What special wonders have you seen?

Perhaps a great prince passing by—
his shining sword against the sky,

Who rides a great white horse for hours
And rescues princesses from towers.

# THE MOUSE

I found a mouse
outside the house.
It was quite cold that day.

I wrapped him in a handkerchief,
And brought him in to play.

I rolled the baseball toward him,
He didn't move a bit.
I tried once more to play,
But all he did was sit.

Then Mom came in from shopping,
And stopped and screamed out twice,

And just to put it simply,
Mothers do not like mice.

# PERFECT UNCLE

The time we went to Uncle Fred's,
We went on lots of hikes,
And in between the baseball games,
Were hula hoops and bikes.

He taught us all to be polite,
To say "Thank You" and "Please".
He showed us how they get
The maple syrup from the trees.

He even fed the squirrels by hand,
He knows them all by name.
And when he barbecued outside,
A million people came.

We fell asleep when that was done,
We got so tired from having fun.
When all is done, and all is said,
Everyone loves my Uncle Fred.

## READING UNDERNEATH
## THE TREE

Just you and me
beneath the tree.

Sunset and leaves,
our favorite book.

And with its bubbling murmur near,
The shining water of the brook.

I've seen the pictures every time,
I've read this book
from end to end,

Here safe and sound
under our tree,

I love to read it all again.

# MRS. SMITH'S DOG

Mrs. Smith bought a brand new dog
To guard her little house,

And that new dog is very small—
No bigger than a mouse.

How he could chase off anyone
is not a choice I'd take,

But he is awfully good at barks
And keeps us all awake.

# MY SISTER'S ROOM

My older sister keeps her room "just so",
It's not a place a boy would want to go.

She has her favorite dolls lined up on stands,
And shouts, "Don't touch those dolls with dirty hands."

I offered her a piece of chocolate cake,
And knew at once I'd made a big mistake.
She looked so horrified and full of gloom,
"Do you want crumbs all over in this room?"

Her favorite doll is little Mary Ann—
All dressed in ruffles with her little lamb.
Day after day she's in her tiny chair,
And all she ever does is sit and stare.

I'd rather spend my playing time outdoors,
Without a thought about a dirty floor,

Where I can wear my favorite shoes and shirt,
And never worry once about the dirt.

## PUPPY BIRTHDAY

You can't surprise our puppy, Pete,
He had already grabbed a seat,

And found the cake we tried to hide
Before we even came inside.

So we sat down to celebrate
And passed around the birthday plates,

He sat there like the Puppy King
And waited for us all to sing.

# HALLOWEEN NIGHT

We waited till the sun went down—
A pirate, princess, and a clown.

Then with a million other feet,
We headed down the darkened street.

Some people hide behind their door
And turn the lights off when you come.

Sometimes you climb a hundred steps,
To get a single piece of gum.

It really is no easy task
To be the kid behind the mask.

But back at home, with tired feet,
And after all the fun,

You pour all of the candy out
And count your treasures, one by one.

# VIEW FROM A TREE

Up in the tree
I can see far and wide,
Beyond the fences here
and far away—
To secret lands where other children play.

These other children
dress so differently,
And speak a language
Not at all like me.

Though some of them are short
and some are tall,
The world is big enough
To hold us all.

And yet I know
We share things from afar—
The friends we love,

And wishing on a star.

## PIRATES

Blue waves crushed in upon the ship,
And crashing in from every side,
We sailed into the pirate cove,
Against the angry ocean tide.

Then Captain John called "Land Ahoy"
And "Victory Complete",
And it was almost noon by then—
Mom called us in to eat.

# ALL OF THE BIRDS

God must have liked the birds a lot,
He made so many kinds:

Bluebirds that sit on windowsills
and tell us that it's Spring,
And fuzzy little chickens
with tiny yellow wings.

And seagulls flying in the sun
Above the beach where children run.
And roosters sitting proud and tall
Who welcome sunrise with their call.

The wise owls watching over things,
and hummingbirds with whirring wings,
that move so fast you cannot blink,
And the flamingos all in pink.

I believe that other birds must fly
Somewhere in heaven's perfect sky.

## BABY'S FIRST STEP

They made a big old fuss today
Because the baby took a step,
My Daddy got his camera out,
My mother almost wept.

Now I go walking every day,
And get myself all dressed,
And if I walked to China—
No one would be impressed.

# PIANO LESSONS

My sister plays piano,
and it isn't any fun
to hear my mother say,
"Once more! Now play another one."

My grandma cries
And says she hasn't heard a song so sweet.
My brother and my good friend Tom
are squirming in their seats.

My Dad knows how to answer,
after listening all night.
He smiles at my Mom and says,
"Yes, that's a song alright!"

# THE TOY SAILBOAT

I put the little sailboat in,
And sent it on its way.
I don't know where the winds will blow,
The river's on its way.

So just keep looking every day,
Because, you know, I warned ya!
By now it may be in New York
Or even California.

# MY PRAYER IN CHURCH

I told God thank you for the snow
We sled down in December.

I said that school's harder now
than last year. I remember.

I like His colored windows
that make rainbows in the air,
And how the people smile and sing
Each time that we are there.

I like the way the candles
flicker when we pass,
Because it looks like fireflies
alive behind the glass.

Sometimes I tiptoe here inside
when there's a moment free.
"Dear God, my name is Johnny,
I hope you remember me."

# WAITING FOR THE RAIN TO STOP

On week days in the classroom,
We can watch the rain come down.
We're warm and snug inside,
And we have all our friends around.

Today the clouds are endless—
I hear the sound of rain,
And all the world is waiting
Outside my windowpane.

Today my friends are all at home,
I'm waiting here to play.
I wouldn't mind the rain at all
If it weren't Saturday.

# EARLY MORNING

In all the world that morning,
I was the only one.
Outside like little mouths,
The buttercups were full of sun.

I saw the milkman in his truck.
I saw the birds wake in their nests.
I saw the roses open up—
I think I like the red ones best.

Alive and restless in their hives,
I heard the buzz of waking bees,
And when I reached the picket fence,
A kite flew high above the trees.

And as I reached the distant hill,
The hawk was flying high and free.
I cannot stop; I cannot rest—
I have a whole wide world to see.

# TAKING A BATH

When little brother takes a bath,
He brings his toys that float,
And fills the bath with ducks and trucks
And plastic sailboats.

It is a wonder he gets clean.
With bubbles to the rim,
and all the toys, and all his noise,
There's hardly room for him.

# PLANTING MY GARDEN

I have to tuck this little plant
into the ground just right,

And place it here with all its friends
To grow into the light.

And when someday it's strong enough
As springtime passes by,

Its roots will rest in solid ground,
And grow up toward the sky.

By then, it might recall this day
Growing so happily,

And by that time it might grow up
To be as big as me.

# IN THE HOSPITAL

We walked down the long hallway.
We didn't say a word—
Nurses walked by in small white hats
That looked a lot like birds.

And it was very quiet.
We found the room was there,
With *"Welcome Katherine"* on the sign—
Pink ribbons everywhere.

I thought at first that we were lost,
And somehow we had missed her,
But there was Mama smiling
And my brand-new baby sister.

## MISTAKEN WORDS

Little Jim had his little pail,
And said, "I'm going to find some whales."
I saw his bucket leaked a bit,
And told him they would never fit.

Later he came running by,
Waving his hands into the sky.
I saw his look of sheer delight,
And knew I hadn't heard him right.

I looked inside to see the whales.
He had a bucketful of snails.

# WAITING FOR SANTA

I have been waiting here all night
To hear his sleigh-bells in the snow—
High over rooftops, near the stars
Where snowy breezes blow.

I hope he has a special map
To find the little girls and boys,
And that his sled is strong enough
To carry all the Christmas toys.

Right now he must be looking down,
And very tired from his ride.
I hope that when he gets here
He will tiptoe here inside.

By then I'll hide myself in bed,
And leave a note from me,
And in the kitchen, just for him—
Some cookies and some tea.

Printed in the United States
By Bookmasters